YouNance Financial Literacy for Youth

YOUNANCE

YOUTH FINANCIAL LITERARY

YouNance Financial Literacy for Youth: Empowering Better Choices for a Brighter Future

Elementary School Workbook

By Pearl A. Fobi

PurposeHouse Publishing

Published by PurposeHouse Publishing, Columbia, Maryland.

Cover Design by PurposeHouse Publishing, www.purposehousepublishing.com

Printed in the USA.

12 11 10 09 08 07 5

ISBN: 978-1-957190-21-1

Contents

List of Illustrations

About YouNance: Mission and Vision

At YouNance, our mission is to empower children with the financial literacy skills necessary to navigate their financial futures with confidence and success. We believe financial education should be accessible to all, regardless of socio-economic status. Our vision is to create a future where every child understands the value of money, the importance of saving, and the potential of investing, ultimately leading to greater financial independence and stability for families in our communities.

Our Team

The YouNance team comprises a diverse group of professionals, including:

- *Financial Educators:* Experts with backgrounds in banking and finance who are passionate about teaching financial concepts.
- *Curriculum Developers:* Educators with experience in K-12 education who design age-appropriate learning materials.
- *Community Advocates:* Individuals committed to promoting financial literacy within underserved communities, ensuring every child can learn and grow.
- *Advisory Board:* A group of financial professionals and educators who provide ongoing insights and feedback to keep our materials relevant and effective.

Contact Information

For further inquiries, feedback, or to share your experiences with the YouNance program, please contact us at learn.younance@gmail.com.

We value your input and look forward to collaborating with families and educators to enhance financial literacy for all students. Your participation is key to cultivating a financially savvy generation!

Introduction: How to Use this Workbook

Purpose of Workbook/Curriculum Levels

The YouNance team designed this workbook to serve as a comprehensive resource for teaching financial literacy to elementary school students. Each section facilitates understanding through relatable scenarios and interactive learning methods.

Purpose

- *To Educate:* Introduce essential financial concepts in a way that resonates with students' everyday lives.
- *To Engage:* Foster an interactive learning environment where students can collaboratively discuss and explore financial topics.
- *To Empower:* Equip students with the knowledge and skills to make informed financial decisions, ultimately instilling confidence and responsibility toward money management.

Elementary Curriculum Level (Grades 3-5)

Focus Areas: The elementary level focuses on basic budgeting, saving, understanding needs versus wants, and the concept of earning money.

Learning Objectives:

- Identify different sources of income.
- Understand the importance of saving for future goals.
- Differentiate between needs and wants.

How to Use This Workbook

This curriculum includes ten weekly case studies for group discussion and individual exploration. There are suggested activities for each case study, and the following suggested classroom instruction sequence can be modified or adapted.

Class Participation: Each case study is designed for group discussion. Encourage students to share their thoughts and experiences related to the scenarios presented. This collaborative approach helps build communication skills and reinforces learning.

Individual Reflection: After group discussions, students should complete *Section A* by answering open-ended questions. Encourage them to think critically and relate the material to their own lives. This reflection will deepen their understanding and retention of the concepts.

Vocabulary Building: *Section B* includes a word match activity that introduces key financial terms. Students should work in pairs or small groups to match terms with their definitions. Discussing these terms as a class will enhance vocabulary retention and comprehension.

Engaging Activities: *Section C* features fun word puzzles related to the case studies. These activities serve as a light-hearted way to reinforce learning. Encourage students to work on these puzzles during class or as homework.

Parent Involvement: To strengthen the learning experience, we encourage parents to engage with their children during the workbook activities. We recommend setting aside time each week for families to discuss what they've learned. Feedback from parents is invaluable; we welcome insights into how to improve the workbook for future editions.

YOUNANCE FINANCIAL LITERACY

Case Study 1: John Doe's First Financial Lesson

Once upon a time, in a cheerful little neighborhood, a ten-year-old boy named John had a big dream: he wanted a shiny new PlayStation 5 for Christmas! But there was one little hiccup. This amazing gaming console cost $500 plus tax, and John didn't have any money saved up. Instead of giving up, John came up with a brilliant idea: why not sell trash bags and help clean up his neighborhood? It was a win-win! But there was just one problem—John needed money to buy the trash bags first. With determination in his heart, he decided it was time to ask his mom for help. What would she say?

JOHN*:* Mom, I really want to buy a PlayStation 5 for Christmas! It costs $500 plus tax.

MOM (JANICE): That's a lot of money, John. How do you want to pay for it?

JOHN: I have an idea! I want to sell trash bags and clean up the neighborhood to earn money. But I need $50 to buy trash bags, gloves, and the other equipment that comes with it. Can you lend me $50?

MOM: Hmm. . .I can lend you the money, but you'll need to do some planning first.

JOHN: Planning? What is that?

MOM: Well, you'll need to list the things you will need and then search for the prices online. It is called budgeting. Go to Walmart.com and figure out how to spend the $50. Once you have that planned, I'll lend you the money. But you'll also have to pay me back.

JOHN: Why will I pay you back? You are my mom.

MOM: That is the first lesson I want to teach you about business. Whenever you borrow money from someone, you must learn to pay it back. That helps build a healthy relationship. Remember, the person asking for the money is the borrower, and the person considering or agreeing to give the money is the lender, and it is called a loan.

JOHN: Okay, so how should I pay you back?

MOM: You have two choices. First, you can use the money you make from your business to pay me back. Or I can take it from your monthly allowance—the money you earn for doing chores and getting good grades.

JOHN: Okay, that sounds fair. I'll work on my plan right now!

Mom: One more thing—if you decide to go ahead with this plan, we'll need to sign a contract. A contract is a written agreement between two people that shows what each person has agreed to do. Without a signed contract, it's just words—no proof, no point. That way, we both understand the deal, and there won't be any confusion later. We'll both sign it before the loan starts.

Later that evening, John talked to his dad, James, about his idea.

JOHN: Dad, guess what! Mom said she'll lend me $50 to start my trash bag business so I can buy a PlayStation 5.

DAD (JAMES): That's interesting, but I think there's a safer way to earn money.

JOHN: Safer? Like what?

DAD: Instead of starting a business right now, you could do more chores around the house to earn extra money. I'll even add an extra $10 to your weekly chores if you wake up before 6 a.m., keep the house clean, and get good grades in school. That way, you can start your own business with your own money. Beginning your own business with a loan is not a good idea.

JOHN: Hmm . . . that sounds like a lot of work, but I can try.

DAD: Remember the story I told you last night about the race between the rabbit and the tortoise? This is an excellent time to apply the slow and steady principle. If you go for that, I'll support you. I'll even get you a piggy bank and a notebook or a jotter to help you save and keep track of your money.

JOHN: Thanks, Dad! I'll think about it and decide soon.

Learning Objectives

1. Understand the concept of saving and setting financial goals. Students will learn how to save money over time to buy something they really want.
2. Identify the roles of borrower and lender. Students will be able to define who the borrower is and who a lender is in a financial situation.
3. Explore the basics of budgeting and price comparison. Students will practice listing needed items, researching costs, and planning how to use a set amount of money.
4. Recognize different ways to earn money. Students will discuss options like doing chores or starting a simple business to earn money.
5. Learn the importance of repaying loans and financial responsibility. Students will understand why paying back borrowed money builds trust and responsibility.

Discussion Questions

Understanding the Situation:

1. Why did John need money, and what was his business idea?
2. What were the two options John had to earn the money?
3. Which of John's two options do you think is better? Why?
4. What are the pros and cons of borrowing money from his mom versus earning more by doing extra chores?
5. If you were John, what would you decide to do, and why?
6. How can John ensure he doesn't spend the $50 loan on other things?
7. What is the most exciting part of John's business idea?
8. Why do you think John's mom and dad gave him different advice?
9. What things do you think John should buy with the $50 to start his business?

10. How can John make sure he saves some money for the PlayStation?
11. Why is it important for John to work hard and repay the loan?
12. How can a piggy bank help John with his goal?

Section A: Individual Reflection

Reflective and Lesson-Oriented Questions: Learning from Experience:

1. What lesson do you think John will learn from this experience?
2. How could John use what he learns here to make better financial decisions in the future?

Values and Goals:

3. Why is it important to save money before spending it? iv) How can setting goals like John's PlayStation help motivate you to work harder?

Parental Advice:

4. Do you think John's mom or dad gave better advice? Why?
5. How do parents and family members influence how we think about money?

Section B: Vocabulary Building

Matching Puzzle: In the answer column, first write the number and put the correct letters to the side, e.g., 2C.

Words	*Definitions*	*Answers*
A) Budget	1) Money you get regularly for doing chores	
B) Loan	2) A small container to hold coins	
C) Save	3) The money you borrow and must return	
D) Allowance	4) A plan for spending money	
E) Piggybank	5) To put money aside for the future	
F) Business	6) Obtain funds from another party with an agreement to repay	
G) Money	7) To use money to buy goods and/or services	
H) Chores	8) An organization engaged in commercial, industrial, or professional activities	
I) Spend	9) A medium of exchange used for transactions and trade	
J) Borrow	10) Routine tasks or duties, typically related to household maintenance	
K) Plan	11) Money owed to another party because of borrowing	
L) Goal	12) Accessible via the internet or connected to a network	
M) Debt	13) A detailed proposal for achieving specific goals or objectives	
N) Online	14) A desired result a person aims to achieve	

Section C: Activities

Word Search Puzzle: Find and circle the financial words hidden in the grid below. Words can go horizontally, vertically, or diagonally.

Z	I	P	I	G	G	Y	B	A	N	K	I
E	B	O	R	R	O	W	U	I	H	K	O
A	U	I	U	N	A	P	L	A	N	B	L
R	D	H	W	O	L	C	O	S	T	U	K
N	G	F	E	I	S	S	A	V	E	S	J
D	E	C	I	S	I	O	N	I	U	I	P
B	T	A	X	P	S	V	O	K	U	N	A
I	Y	D	Y	E	A	I	M	O	N	E	Y
U	U	H	O	N	L	I	N	E	Y	S	M
Y	B	U	O	D	E	B	T	K	K	S	E
C	H	O	R	E	S	E	I	L	O	P	N
K	O	A	L	L	O	W	A	N	C	E	T

Budget	Debt
Loan	Piggybank
Save	Borrow
Spend	Online
Sale	Decision
Debt	Chores
Business	Earn
Allowance	Payment
Money	Tax
Plan	Cost
Goal	

Alternative Activities

1. Creative Task: Design a flyer or ad for John's trash bag cleaning business. What would you include to attract customers?
2. Roleplay: Imagine you are John. Present your business plan to your class as if it is your mom or dad.
3. Group Discussion**:** Divide into two groups: One group supports John borrowing money, and the other supports him earning it through chores. Debate which option is better.

This case study emphasizes the importance of paying back borrowed money, understanding profit, and saving for things you want to buy.

Case Study 2: A Conversation at the Dinner Table

In a cozy home filled with laughter and love, Mrs. Johnson, a dedicated single mother, had three wonderful children: Sam, a high school senior with big dreams; Brian, a curious middle schooler; and little Sophia, who was just starting elementary school. One evening, after a delicious dinner, Mrs. Johnson gathered her kids around the table for a special talk. This wasn't just any chat—it was about money! She wanted to share important lessons on how to make smart choices with their finances. With excitement in the air, the children leaned in, eager to learn how to be wise with their money and take charge of their futures. What valuable lessons would they discover together?

Mrs. Johnson's Story

"Sam," Mrs. Johnson started, "now that you've got your first job, it is important we open a bank account for you. My goal is to ensure you make the most of your money. You'll be heading to college soon, so this is the perfect time to learn some important lessons."

Sam nodded. He liked the idea of earning his own money but wasn't sure how to manage it.

"First, let's talk about how to ensure you know what to do when you get paid," Mrs. Johnson said. "Sam, you need to know that a budget isn't a way to stop you from spending money. A budget is like a map—it helps you tell your money where to go so you're not left wondering where it went."

Brian asked, "Why is a budget so important?"

Mrs. Johnson smiled. "Let's say Sam gets paid $500 from his job. If he doesn't plan, he might spend $100 on snacks, $200 on clothes, and $300 on video games. Then, when he needs gas for the car or must buy school supplies, he won't have enough. A budget makes sure he saves first and spends wisely."

Sophia raised her hand. "What if something bad happens?"

"That's why we save for emergencies," Mrs. Johnson said. "If Sam has an emergency fund, he won't need to borrow money or overdraft his account. Did you know that when you spend more than you have in your bank account, the bank charges you extra fees? It's like borrowing money you didn't plan to borrow, and it can add up fast."

"Wow," Sam said. "I didn't know that. So, what should I do with my paycheck?"

Mrs. Johnson replied, "Before you spend a single dollar, plan. Save some of it for your future, use some for your needs, and you can spend a little on fun stuff, too. And remember, always stay away from people who might lead you to make bad choices. Did you know that many crimes and drug problems start with the wrong crowd? Making good decisions now will help you have a bright future."

Learning Objectives

1. Understand the purpose of a budget. Students will learn that a budget is a helpful plan to manage money wisely, not something that stops them from spending.
2. Recognize the importance of saving for emergencies. Students will understand that setting aside money can help during unexpected situations.
3. Identify needs vs. wants when spending money. Students will learn to tell the difference between things they need (like school supplies) and things they want (like video games).
4. Explore the idea of earning money and making smart choices with it. Students will see how working for money brings responsibility, and they'll learn how to make good decisions about spending and saving.
5. Learn about avoiding financial mistakes like overdraft fees. Students will be introduced to the idea that spending more than you have can lead to extra charges and problems.

Discussion Questions

1. Why is it important to plan for your money?
2. What is an emergency fund, and how can it help?
3. Why should you stay away from the wrong crowd?
4. What does it mean to overdraft your bank account?
5. Why is it a good idea to save money before spending it?
6. How can a piggy bank or a jar help you save?
7. What is something you might save for?

Section A: Individual Reflection

1. How will saving money now help you in the future?
2. Why is it important to think before spending?
3. What would you do if you found yourself running out of money too quickly?
4. What advice would you give a friend about managing money?

Section B: Vocabulary Building

Matching Puzzle: In the answer column, first write the number and put the correct letters to the side, e.g., 2C.

Definitions	*Words*	*Answers*
1)A plan that helps you manage your money	a) Emergency	
2)Setting money aside for the future	b) Paycheck	
3) An unexpected event that you need to prepare for financially	c)Bank	
4)The money you earn from work	d)Fees (Overdraft)	
5)A place where your money is stored safely	e) Budget	
6) Extra charges when you spend more than what you have in your account	f) Save	
7) The money you get for working or doing a job	g) Priorities	
8) To use money to buy something	h) job	
9) A place where you keep your money for savings, spending, or investment purposes	i) Spend	
10) The most important thing you choose to do first	j) Earnings	
11) Work that a person does to earn money	k) Personal Account	
12) Choosing among many options on how to use your money	l)Map	
13) A smart way to use your money	m)Choices	
14) A guide that helps us reach our money goal	n) plan	
15) Picking how to use our money	o) decision	

Section C: Activities

Word Search Puzzle: Find and circle the financial words hidden in the grid below. Words can go horizontally, vertically, or diagonally.

S	E	R	P	A	Y	C	H	E	C	K	U	B			
P	F	M	J	O	B	H	R	P	F	U	B	O		**Charges**	**Job**
R	I	O	D	E	E	A	O	L	C	Y	U	R		**Earn**	**Bank**
I	N	N	S	D	A	R	V	A	D	T	D	O		**Finances**	**Priorities**
O	A	E	M	E	R	G	E	N	C	Y	G	W		**Smart**	**Overdraft**
R	N	Y	A	C	N	E	R	B	H	S	E	F		**Fees**	**Choices**
I	C	S	R	I	E	S	D	A	O	A	T	U		**Save**	**Future**
T	E	P	T	S	D	R	R	N	I	V	T	T		**Borrow**	**Spend**
I	S	E	U	I	A	E	A	K	C	E	F	U		**Plan**	**Decision**
E	E	N	Y	O	F	R	F	E	E	S	D	R		**Emergency**	**Peak**
S	D	d	E	N	U	T	T	F	S	D	E	E		**Money**	**Paycheck**

Alternative Activities

1. Pretend you're planning for a family day out. Work together to make a budget for food, tickets, and other expenses. Decide how much to save and how much to spend.
2. Draw or decorate your own piggy bank on paper. Write down something you'd like to save for inside the piggy bank.

This case study encourages meaningful discussions and practical activities, making financial literacy relatable for all age groups.

Case Study 3: Learning Financial Lessons as a Family

The Story: Joshua and Evelyn Teach Their Kids About Money

Joshua and Evelyn had a warm and caring home, but they were facing a tough time. With Joshua's work hours cut back, making ends meet had become a challenge for their family of four, including their spirited thirteen-year-old son, Daniel, and their imaginative eight-year-old daughter, Sara. One evening, as the sun set and the kitchen filled with the comforting aroma of dinner, the family gathered around the table for an important discussion. They knew it was time to come together and brainstorm ways to manage their money better. With determination in their hearts, they shared ideas and listened to one another, ready to tackle their financial challenges as a team. What solutions would they come up with to help their family thrive?

The Dinner Table Conversation

DANIEL: "Mom, why can't you buy me the new game console?"

EVELYN: "Dan, it's not that we don't want to buy nice things. We have to pay for what's most important first. Things like food (groceries), rent, gas, bills, and utilities. Those are needs. A game console is something we want, but it's not something we need."

SARA: "What's the difference between needs and wants?"

JOSHUA: "Needs are things we can't live without, like food, water, and a roof over our heads, often called shelter. Wants are things we'd like to have but can live without. What do you think is more important—buying groceries or getting the console?"

SARA: "Groceries."

EVELYN: "Exactly. But if we save carefully, we might be able to afford some of the things we want later."

Learning to Prioritize

Joshua pulled out a notepad. "Let's make a list," he said. "First, we'll write down everything we spend money on, and then we'll figure out what's most important." *Here's what they wrote down:*

Needs (4 Walls)	**Wants**
Rents	Vacation
Groceries	Game Console
Utilities	Shopping
Clothing	Movie Nights

JOSHUA: "We need to pay for the needs first. But we can still plan for the wants by budgeting."

The 50/30/20 Rule

Evelyn explained, "The 50/30/20 rule is a way to divide our money:

- 50% for Needs, like rent and groceries.
- 30% for Wants, like the game console or the movies.
- 20% for Savings, so we're ready for emergencies."

She drew a pie chart to show how it works: If the family has $1,000, then $500 goes to needs, $300 to wants, and $200 to savings

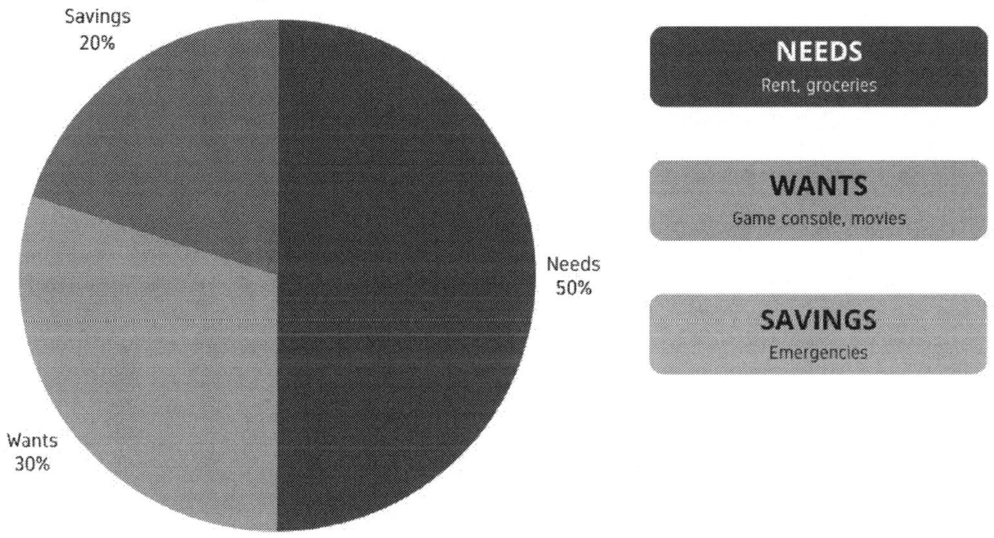

Figure 1: 50/30/20 Rule

DANIEL: "So, if we save $200 a month, we'd have $2,400 in a year?"

JOSHUA: "Exactly! And if something unexpected happens, like a car repair, we'll be ready."

EVELYN: "It's like preparing for a storm. If we don't save, we'd have to borrow money for things like fixing the roof or buying medicine, which makes life harder. But if we save little by little, we'll be ready for surprises."

SARA: "Like keeping an umbrella for a rainy day!

EVELYN: "Exactly. If we avoid spending on things we don't need, we can still enjoy fun things later, like going to the movies."

JOSHUA: "Planning our money isn't about saying no to fun. It's about making sure we take care of what matters first. That way, we can enjoy what we want without worry." Daniel: "I get it now. Saving is like making sure we're ready for the future."

EVELYN & JOSHUA: Absolutely!

Learning Objectives

1. Understand the difference between needs and wants. Students will learn how to tell what things are important to have (like food and shelter) and what things are just nice to have (like games and vacations).
2. Recognize the importance of prioritizing spending. Students will explore how families decide what to pay for first and why essentials come before extras.
3. Learn how to budget using the 50/30/20 rule. Students will be introduced to a simple way to divide money: 50% for needs, 30% for wants, and 20% for savings.
4. Understand the value of saving for emergencies. Students will see why saving money "for a rainy day" helps families handle unexpected problems without borrowing.
5. Appreciate teamwork and family decision-making in money matters. Students will understand how discussing money as a family can help everyone make smart financial choices together.

Discussion Questions

1. What are "needs," and what are "wants"? Can you name an example of each?
2. Why is it important to plan how we spend our money?
3. What does the 50/30/20 rule mean?
4. Why should we save money for emergencies?
5. How do savings help us prepare for unexpected expenses?
6. Can you list some things you need and something you want?
7. Why do you think it's important to buy the things we need first?
8. If you had $100, how much would you save to prepare for a rainy day?
9. What fun thing could you buy if you saved it?
10. How would you feel if you saved enough money to buy a special toy or gift?

Section A: Individual Reflection

1. What is the most important thing you learned from the story?
2. How can you help your family save money at home?
3. What would you like to save for in the future?

Section B: Vocabulary Building

Matching Puzzle: In the answer column, first write the number and put the correct letters to the side, e.g., 2C.

Definitions	*Words*	*Answers*
A. Money set aside for the future	1) Budget	
B. Things like rent, food, and utilities	2) Savings	
C. Unexpected events that require extra money	3) Needs	
D. Something you'd like but can live without	4) Wants	
E. A plan to manage your spending	5) Emergencies	
F. Amount of money we owe for services like electricity and paid regularly	6) Priorities	
G. A set of steps we decide to follow to reach our goal or complete a task	7) Shelter	
H. To fix something that is broken or not working properly	8) Utilities	
I. Use money to buy things or pay for services	9) Bills	
J. A safe place where you live that protects you from weather and keeps you comfortable	10) Rainy-day Fun	
K. Instruction that tells us what we should or shouldn't do	11) Plan	
L. Things you must have to live, like food and a house	12) Spend	
M. Money saved for unexpected situations	13) Repair	
N. The most important things you need to do first before anything else	14) Rule	

Section C: Activities

Word Search Puzzle: Find and circle the financial words hidden in the grid below. Words can go horizontally, vertically, or diagonally.

S	P	G	R	O	C	E	R	I	E	S	Y	O			
H	R	E	P	A	I	R	B	U	D	G	E	T		Needs	Rainy-day
E	I	C	O	N	S	O	L	E	T	N	E	U		Wants	Vacation
L	O	E	W	R	A	M	O	V	I	E	S	T		Shelter	Movies
T	R	R	A	I	N	Y	D	A	Y	E	H	I		Saving	List
E	I	L	N	P	L	A	N	C	V	D	E	L		Emergency	Puzzle
R	T	I	T	U	Z	I	O	A	X	S	L	I		Plan	Budget
V	Y	S	S	Z	I	O	N	T	T	U	T	T		Future	Groceries
R	A	T	E	Z	S	A	V	I	N	G	E	I		Utilities	Bills
U	B	I	L	L	S	E	T	O	N	Y	R	E		Spend	Console
L	C	E	M	E	R	G	E	N	C	Y	E	S		Priorities	Repair
E	F	U	T	U	R	E	S	P	E	N	D	U		Shelter	Rule

Alternative Activities

1. Draw a picture of a piggy bank and decorate it. Write down or draw three things you want to save for.
2. Create a chart showing "needs" and "wants" with pictures from magazines or drawings.

This case study emphasizes the importance of prioritizing needs over wants when planning how to spend money.

Case Study 4: Gabriel Learns About Banking

The Story

Gabriel, an adventurous 11-year-old in 5th grade, was buzzing with excitement as he received a new assignment from his teacher: learn about what your parents do for work! His dad, Mr. Taylor, worked at a bank, but Gabriel wasn't quite sure what that really meant. As he thought about the upcoming week of research and presentations, a mix of excitement and nervousness filled him. That evening, he decided to take the plunge and sat down with his dad at the kitchen table, eager to unravel the mysteries of banking. With a notebook in hand and curiosity in his heart, Gabriel was ready to ask questions and discover the fascinating world of his dad's job. What surprising things would he learn about the life of a banker?

The Conversation with Dad

"Dad, my teacher gave us a project to learn about what our parents do. So. . . what do you do at the bank?"

Mr. Taylor smiled and said, "That's a great question, Gabriel. Let me explain it simply. A bank is a place where people keep their money safe. It also helps people save money, pay bills, borrow money when needed, and much more. My job is to help people manage their money and make smart decisions." "What do you mean by keeping money safe?" Gabriel asked.

"Well," his dad replied, "imagine if you kept all your money at home in a jar. It could get lost, stolen, or damaged. At the bank, we keep it secure. And with online banking, people can access their money on their phones or computers, so they don't always have to come into the bank."

"Wow! I didn't know you could do that," Gabriel said. "So, can anyone open an account?"

"Yes," Mr. Taylor said. "At the bank, we help people open savings and checking accounts. A savings account is for putting money away for later, like a piggy bank, but it earns extra money called interest. A savings account used to earn high interest but not as much anymore. Now the banks encourage people to invest their money. A checking account is for spending money on things you need now, like groceries or bills."

Gabriel nodded. "What about checks? I've heard of them but don't really understand how they work."

"Good question! A check is like a note you write to tell the bank to pay someone money from your account. Here, let me show you."

Mr. Taylor pulled out a check and explained the parts.

The Parts of a Check

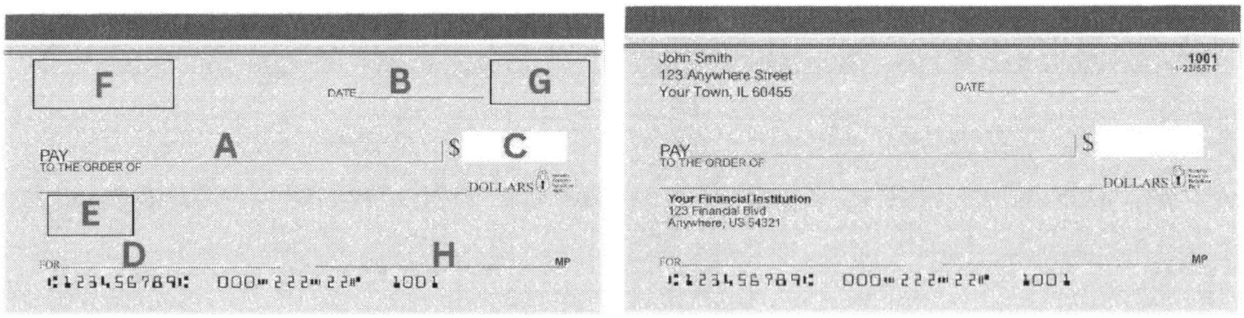

Figure 2: The Parts of a Check

(A) The name of the person or company receiving the money.

(B) The date.

(C) The amount of money written in numbers

(D) Memo: Purpose for the check.

(E) Name of Banking Institution

(F) Name and Address of the Check Issuer

(G) Check Number (To confirm during an audit)

(H) Signature of the Person Issuing the Check.

(I) It will be at the back of the check for the person receiving to sign an agreement to the amount and authorize the bank to pay them that amount from Person F's account.

"Cool!" Gabriel said. "Can we write a check together sometime?"

"Of course! When it is time to pay the bills, I will have you sit down with me so we can do it together. Also, when you're older, I'll help you open your own account," Mr. Taylor said proudly.

Learning Objectives

1. Understand what a bank does and why it is important. Students will learn that banks help keep money safe, and allow people to save, spend, and manage their finances.
2. Recognize the difference between a savings account and a checking account. Students will explore how savings accounts are used to save money and earn interest while checking accounts are used for everyday spending.
3. Identify the basic parts of a check and their purposes. Students will be introduced to the key components of a check and how they are used to paying others.
4. Explore how technology like online banking helps manage money. Students will understand that money can be accessed safely using devices like phones and computers, not just at the bank.
5. Learn the role of bankers and how they help people with their money. Students will gain insight into what bankers do and how they support individuals in making smart financial decisions.

Discussion Questions

1. What is a bank, and why is it important?
2. What are the differences between a savings account and a checking account?
3. What is a check, and how is it used?

4. What is online or mobile banking?
5. How does a bank help people manage their money?
6. Why do people keep money in a bank instead of at home?
7. What does a savings account help you do?
8. Can you describe one thing you learned about a check? I) Why is it important to keep money safe?
9. What's one fun thing you'd save for in a savings account?

Section A: Individual Reflection

1. What did you learn about how banks keep money safe?
2. How do you think a savings account can help you in the future?
3. What would you save if you had your own account?

Section B: Vocabulary Building

Matching Puzzle: In the answer column, first write the number and put the correct letters to the side, e.g., 2C.

Definitions	*Words*	*Answers*
A. A place that keeps money safe and helps us save, spend, and/or borrow	1) Check Drawer	
B. A written promise to pay someone money from your bank account	2) Check Drawee	
C. Extra money paid for borrowing or earned from savings	3) Savings Account	
D. Payments we make for things like electricity, water, phone bills, etc.	4) Checking Account	
E. Choosing the best way to use our money wisely	5) Interest	
F. A person who writes and signs a check to pay someone	6) Smart Decision	
G. A bank that pays the money when a check is cashed or deposited	7) Online Banking	
H. Using the internet to manage your money in any of your accounts	8) A Check	
I. A bank account used for everyday spending, such as paying bills	9) Bills	
J. A safe place in a bank to store money and earn interest over time	10) Bank	
K. A person who works at a bank assisting customers	12) Banker	

Section C: Activities

Word Search Puzzle: Find and circle the financial words hidden in the grid below. Words can go horizontally, vertically, or diagonally.

F	U	T	U	R	E	P	R	E	S	E	N	T
D	I	S	C	O	V	E	R	W	O	R	K	N
C	O	M	P	A	N	Y	D	A	C	I	O	E
A	B	A	N	K	A	Z	A	L	O	N	P	R
T	A	S	S	I	G	N	M	E	N	T	I	V
D	N	T	E	C	D	E	A	A	V	E	G	O
R	K	O	C	F	G	H	G	R	E	R	G	U
A	E	L	U	I	J	K	E	N	R	E	Y	S
W	R	E	R	B	I	L	L	S	S	S	B	P
E	V	N	E	C	H	E	C	K	A	T	A	R
E	S	A	V	I	N	G	S	A	T	O	N	O
C	H	E	C	K	I	N	G	T	I	I	K	J
D	R	A	W	E	R	E	X	L	O	S	T	E
S	I	G	N	A	T	U	R	E	N	E	E	C

Assignment	**Banker**
Conversation	**Bank**
Lost	**Stolen**
Damage	**Secure**
Savings	**Checking**
Piggybank	**Interest**
Check	**Signature**
Drawer	**Drawee**
Company	**Decision**
Bills	**Learn**
Discover	**Present**
Future	**Nervous**
Project	**Work**

Alternative Activities

1. Draw a picture of a bank and write three things a bank helps people do.
2. Practice "writing" a pretend check to a friend or family member for something fun.

Case Study 5: Tatiana's Family Financial Talk

Tatiana, a dedicated Nurse Practitioner and single mom of four—Simon (18), Dominic (16), George (15), and Anna (14)—had always worked tirelessly to provide for her children. One day, the siblings came home after an unfair experience at school. They witnessed George being laughed at by his rich classmates for not having all his school supplies. It was time to learn about money. They wanted to be smart about working, saving, and watching their money grow for the future. Recognizing the importance of this journey, Tatiana invited Julius, a retired financial advisor and beloved elder from their church, to join their family discussion. With excitement in the air, the siblings gathered around the table, ready to soak up wisdom and take the first steps toward financial independence. What valuable lessons would Julius share that could shape their financial future?

The Conversation

SIMON: "Mom, I want to take a part-time job at the coffee shop near school, but I'm concerned about balancing it with my classes and sports. What do you think?

TATIANA: "That's a great question, Simon. I think part-time work can teach you responsibility, but you'll need to plan your time carefully. Julius, what advice do you have?"

JULIUS: "Simon, working part-time is a great way to learn about managing money and your time. Let's do this: start with fewer hours, maybe weekends, and make sure your grades and activities don't suffer. Then, you can adjust your schedule if needed.

DOMINIC: "I'd like to work too, but I don't want my grades to drop. How can I save money without a job?"

TATIANA: "You don't need a job right away to save. You can start small, like cutting back on things you don't need or helping with tasks at home for a little allowance. Julius?"

JULIUS: "That's right. You could also try a small money-making project at home, like selling something you make or doing yard work for neighbors. Every little bit you save adds up over time."

GEORGE: "I really want to start a business, but I don't know which idea to pick: photography, social media content creation, cleaning service, or car washing. How do I figure it out?"

TATIANA: "Starting a business is a big step, George. I'm proud of you for thinking about it. Julius, what advice would you give him?"

JULIUS: "George, think about what you enjoy and what you're good at. For example, if you love photography, start by offering your services for free or at a low cost to family and friends or even to the church. It's okay to try one idea first, learn from it, and move to another if it doesn't work out. Also, look at how much money you'd need to start each idea and how much time you'd have to put in.

ANNA: "I've been saving my birthday money. Can I make it grow instead of just keeping it in my piggy bank?"

JULIUS: "Great question, Anna! When you invest, your money can grow over time instead of just sitting there."

SIMON: "How does that work?"

JULIUS: "Think of investing like planting a tree. You start with a small seed (your money), and over time, it grows bigger. For example, if you buy a tiny part of a company—called a stock—it can become worth more later."

DOMINIC: "So, kids can invest too?"

TATIANA: "Yes! You can start by earning interest in a savings account or having a small investment account with an adult's help."

GEORGE: "What if I want to invest in my own business?"

JULIUS: "That's smart! A business is also an investment. If you work hard and plan well, it can make you more money in the future."

ANNA: "I like that! Where should I start?"

JULIUS: "Start small—maybe save some money in a bank that gives interest or learn about beginner investments. The key is to be patient and make smart choices!"

Learning Objectives

1. Understand the value of earning money through work or helping at home. Students will learn that they can earn money by doing chores, part-time work, or small tasks in their community.
2. Explore simple ways to start saving and making money grow. Students will discover that saving money in a piggy bank, bank account, or investing wisely can help it grow over time.
3. Learn how to choose a business idea based on interests and skills. Students will understand that doing something they enjoy—like photography or cleaning—can be a good start for a small business.
4. Recognize that smart financial planning includes setting goals and being patient. Students will be introduced to the idea that financial success takes time and thoughtful decision-making.
5. Discover that kids can invest and build their own financial future. Students will be encouraged to start small with saving and investing, with help from adults, to prepare for a better future.

Discussion Questions

1. What are some ways you can earn money as a kid?
2. Why is it important to save money before spending it?
3. Why do you think people save money instead of spending it all at once?

Section A: Individual Reflection

1. If you had $100, how would you use it to help your family or save for something special?
2. What's something you can do this week to help your family save money?

Section B: Vocabulary Building

Matching Puzzle: In the answer column, first write the number and put the correct letters to the side, e.g., 2C.

Definitions	*Words*	*Answers*
A. A person who helps others manage their money	**1) Allowance**	
B. Work only for part of the day or the week	**2) Sacrifices**	
C. A nurse with extra training who can treat patients and give medicine	**3) Project**	
D. Doing tasks or jobs to earn money or help others	**4) Financial Advisor**	
E. Money that parents give kids to spend or save	**5) Part-Time**	
F. Money people pay to the government for services like schools and roads	**6) Full-Time**	
G. Small pieces of ownership in a company that you can buy or sell	**7) Nurse Practitioner**	
H. A place where people buy and sell things	**8) Job**	
I. A special task or activity to complete	**9) Work**	
J. Simple or easy to understand	**10) Taxes**	
K. Work people do to earn money	**11) Market**	
L. Working for the whole day, usually five days a week	**12) Stocks**	
M. Giving up something now to get something better later	**13) Basics**	

Section C: Activity

Word Search Puzzle: Find and circle the financial words hidden in the grid below. Words can go horizontally, vertically, or diagonally.

B	U	S	I	N	E	S	S	C	A	P	I	T	A	L	O
A	D	V	I	S	O	R	B	O	M	A	R	K	E	T	P
P	R	O	J	E	C	T	A	W	O	R	K	E	R	T	I
A	E	R	O	Z	S	E	S	E	N	T	A	X	E	S	G
B	S	A	C	R	I	F	I	C	E	T	G	T	A	I	G
C	P	Q	E	R	U	I	C	O	Y	I	R	R	C	B	Y
J	O	B	S	E	R	V	I	C	E	M	A	E	C	L	B
D	N	F	U	L	L	T	I	M	E	E	D	Z	O	I	A
E	S	T	O	C	K	S	S	E	X	U	E	Y	U	N	N
F	I	N	V	E	S	T	M	E	N	T	S	X	N	G	K
G	B	P	H	O	T	O	G	R	A	P	H	Y	T	S	W
A	L	L	O	W	A	N	C	E	S	V	U	T	S	R	Q
H	E	C	O	M	P	A	N	Y	S	A	V	I	N	G	P
I	J	G	U	I	D	A	N	C	E	J	K	L	M	N	O

Sacrifices	**Grades**
Siblings	**Allowances**
Money	**Project**
Responsible	**Work**
Job	**Saving**
Fulltime	**Parttime**
Invest	**Guidance**
Business	**Advisor**
Taxes	**Capital**
Stocks	**Basic**
Market	**Photography**
Services	**Piggybank**
Company	**Account**

YOUNANCE FINANCIAL LITERACY

Case Study 6: Credit, Borrowing, and Buying a Home

Mark, a devoted single dad, was navigating the challenges of raising his three sons—Stephen (17), Ralph (14), and Sam (10)—after the loss of his wife. One day, as they talked about their future, the boys expressed their desire for a stable home and asked Mark about the benefits of buying a house. This sparked a heartfelt family discussion, where Mark took the opportunity to explain the concepts of credit, borrowing, and homeownership in a way that they could all understand. With patience and care, he explained important lessons about financial responsibility, helping his sons grasp the significance of making wise choices. As they shared their thoughts and questions, the family came together, united in hopes for a brighter future. What insights would they uncover during this meaningful conversation?

The Family Conversation

What is Credit? Borrowing and Repaying Money

MARK: I'm thinking about buying a house so we can have more space and stability. To do that, I'll need good credit.

SAM: What's credit?

MARK: Credit is like a trust score. It shows how good you are at paying back borrowed money. If you borrow money and repay it on time, people trust you to borrow again. For example, if you borrow $5 from a friend for candy and pay them back quickly, they'll trust you next time. But if you don't, they might not want to lend it to you again.

RALPH: How do people build credit?

MARK: One way is to use credit cards. There are two types: Secured credit cards: It is called secured because it is your money you put down to use. The bank uses that to study your spending habits and will reward you with more based on how well you handle it. Unsecured credit cards: No deposit is needed from you, but it's riskier since you can borrow more than you can afford.

DIANE (FAMILY FRIEND): If you use a credit card, spend wisely. For example, if you spend $50, pay it off fully by the end of the month. This shows lenders you're responsible.

STEPHEN: What if you don't pay it back?

DIANE: Your FICO score goes down, and the company charges interest—extra money for borrowing. That's why you shouldn't spend more than you can afford to repay.

SAM: What's interest?

MARK: Interest is the extra money you pay for borrowing. If you borrow $100 at 10% interest, you pay back $110. The longer it takes, the more interest you owe. That's why people say debt can steal your future—it takes money you could've used for other things.

STEPHEN: What's a FICO score?

MARK: It's a number from 300 to 850 that shows how trustworthy you are with money. A high score helps you get loans at low interest rates. For example, if I have a high score, the bank might lend me money at 5% interest.

But if my score is low, they might charge 8%, costing me thousands more over time.

DIANE: To build good credit:

- Pay bills on time.
- Use only a small part of your credit card limit.
- Don't apply for too many loans or cards at once.

RALPH: What's a debt trap?

MARK: A debt trap is when someone borrows too much and can't repay it. This happens when people only pay the minimum on credit cards or take new loans to cover old ones.

DIANE: To avoid debt traps, always pay your bills in full when possible and only borrow what you can repay.

MARK: If we manage money wisely, we can achieve big goals like buying a home while staying out of debt.

Learning Objectives

1. Understand what credit is and why it is important. Students will learn that credit is a way to show how responsible someone is with borrowing and repaying money.
2. Recognize how borrowing money works and what interest means. Students will be introduced to the idea that when you borrow money, you may have to pay back more than you borrowed due to interest.
3. Learn the difference between secured and unsecured credit cards. Students will understand that secured cards use their own money as a deposit, while unsecured cards do not, but both must be used wisely.
4. Identify simple ways to build good credit. Students will explore easy habits like paying bills on time and not borrowing too much to help maintain a good credit score.
5. Understand what a debt trap is and how to avoid it. Students will learn that borrowing too much money without a plan to repay it can cause long-term problems, and being smart with money helps prevent that.

Discussion Questions

1. What is credit, and why is it important?
2. What happens if you don't pay back borrowed money?
3. Why is it better to own a home instead of renting?
4. How does interest work, and why is it important to pay off debt quickly?
5. What is borrowing, and why do you need to pay back the money you borrow?
6. Why is it important to save money instead of spending it all?
7. What's the difference between a house and an apartment?

Section A: Individual Reflection

1. Reflective and Lesson-Oriented Questions: Elementary School
2. What's one thing you can do to save money for something important?
3. Why is it important to return something you borrow?

Section B: Vocabulary Building

Matching Puzzle: In the answer column, first write the number and put the correct letters to the side, e.g., 2C.

Definitions	*Words*	*Answers*
A. Credit cards that let you borrow without needing to pay anything upfront	1) Homeownership	
B. Taking something from someone with the promise to give it back late	2) Secured Cards	
C. The ability to borrow money or get things now and pay for them later	3) Unsecured Cards	
D. Money you borrow that must be paid back later, usually with extra fees called interest	4) Benefit	
E. A situation where a person keeps borrowing money, can't pay it back, and it makes their problem worse	5) Afford	
F. Means being steady and not changing or falling apart easily	6) Borrowing	
G. The chance of something bad happening or losing something	7) Credit	
H. Extra money you pay when you borrow or the money you earn when you save	8) Lending	
I. Money you put down to hold something or to open an account, which you can get back later	9) Loans	
J. Owning a house where you live instead of renting	10) Debt Traps	
k. Means to give back the money that you borrowed	11) Trust Score	
L. To need to pay back money that you borrowed from someone	12) Stability	
M. The good things you get from something like help or advantages	13) Risk	
N. A number that shows how reliable someone is with money based on their past behavior	14) Deposits	
O. Giving money or things to someone and expecting them to return it later	15) Owe	
P. Having enough money to buy something	16) Repay	
Q. Credit card that you pay for in advance to help build your credit	17) Interest Rates	

Section C: Activities

Word Search Puzzle: Find and circle the financial words hidden in the grid below. Words can go horizontally, vertically, or diagonally.

T	D	E	P	O	S	I	T	C	H	A	R	G	E	S	D	O	G	E		Plans	Interest
R	U	N	S	E	C	U	R	E	D	M	O	N	E	Y	B	U	L	L		Credit	Trustworthy
U	D	E	C	R	E	D	I	T	E	B	E	N	E	F	I	T	I	E		Borrow	Trap
S	E	D	L	E	N	D	O	I	S	O	D	E	M	A	N	A	G	E		Loan	Payment
T	F	H	O	M	E	O	W	N	E	R	S	H	I	P	T	C	L	C		Purchase	Rents
W	A	N	A	P	Q	R	G	L	C	R	T	E	R	U	E	H	E	O		Stability	Prompts
O	U	W	N	I	U	I	O	O	U	O	A	E	I	R	R	A	N	M		Benefits	Money
R	L	O	N	G	I	S	A	N	R	W	B	Q	S	C	E	R	D	P		Affordability	Repay
T	T	R	A	P	T	K	L	G	E	I	I	I	K	H	S	G	P	A		Homeownership	Payment
H	R	E	P	A	Y	Y	S	I	D	N	L	U	Y	A	T	E	L	N		Equity	Deposits
Y	A	F	F	O	R	D	A	B	I	L	I	T	Y	S	N	S	A	C		Secured	Minimum
O	P	A	Y	M	E	N	T	R	E	N	T	Y	A	E	E	O	N	D		Unsecured	Score
S	C	O	R	E	P	R	O	M	P	T	Y	U	I	O	P	X	E	B		Default	Charges

Alternative Activities

1. Borrow and Repay Game: Give students pretend money to "borrow" and "repay." Discuss why repaying on time is important.
2. Needs vs. Wants Sorting: Provide a list of items and have students sort them into "needs" and "wants."

This case study's family conversation introduces credit and borrowing in a relatable way, teaching students at all levels to understand and manage these financial concepts responsibly.

Case Study 7: Taxes a.k.a. Uncle Sam

One evening, after a delicious family dinner filled with laughter and stories, Debbie and Jake settled down in the cozy living room with their parents, Jamal and Stacy. The lamp's soft glow illuminated their faces as they gathered on the comfortable couch, ready for an important family discussion. Curious and excited, the kids knew this was a special time to connect with their parents and learn something new. What topics would they explore together, and what valuable lessons awaited them in this warm and inviting setting?

DEBBIE: "Mom, Dad, why are you both so busy during certain months of the year? You seem to spend more time working and less time with us."

JAMAL: "That's a great question, Debbie. Those busy months are what we call 'tax season.' It's the time when many people need help preparing and filing their taxes."

JAKE: "What are taxes?"

STACY: "Taxes are money that people and businesses pay to the government. This money helps pay for things we all use, like schools, roads, parks, and hospitals."

DEBBIE: "Why does everyone have to pay taxes?"

JAMAL: "Everyone benefits from the services the government provides. By paying taxes, we all contribute to making our community a better place."

JAKE: "Who has to pay taxes?"

STACY: "Most people who earn money are required to pay taxes. This includes adults who work jobs, own businesses, or make money in other ways. Even our business pays taxes."

DEBBIE: "How are taxes structured?"

JAMAL: "There are different types of taxes. For example:

- Income Tax: A portion of the money people earn goes to the government.
- Sales Tax: When you buy something, a little extra is added to the price as tax.
- Property Tax: People who own houses or land pay a tax for owning it.

JAKE: "What happens if someone doesn't pay their taxes?"

STACY: "If people don't pay their taxes, the government might send reminders or charge extra fees called penalties. In some cases, they can get into serious trouble. That's why it's important to pay taxes on time."

DEBBIE: "When is the latest time to pay taxes?"

JAMAL: "In the U.S., the deadline to file taxes is usually April 15 each year. During this time, we help many people prepare their taxes, so they don't miss the deadline."

JAKE: "So, during tax season, you're helping people make sure they pay their taxes correctly and on time?"

STACY: "Exactly, Jake. By helping others file their taxes, we ensure they follow the law and avoid any penalties."

DEBBIE: "Thanks for explaining, Mom and Dad. We understand why you're so busy during tax season now."

JAMAL: "You're welcome, kids. It's important to know about taxes and how they affect everyone."

Learning Objectives

1. Understand what taxes are and why they are important. Students will learn that taxes are money paid to the government to help fund things like schools, roads, and hospitals.
2. Recognize different types of taxes people may pay. Students will be introduced to income tax, sales tax, and property tax in simple terms they can relate to.
3. Learn who is responsible for paying taxes. Students will understand that most adults who earn money or own property are required to pay taxes.

4. Understand the purpose of tax season and filing deadlines. Students will explore why tax season is a busy time and why it's important to file taxes on time—usually by April 15 in the U.S.
5. Identify the consequences of not paying taxes. Students will learn that failing to pay taxes can lead to penalties or legal trouble, which is why being responsible with taxes matters.

Discussion Questions:

1. What are taxes?
2. Why do people pay taxes?
3. Can you name something that taxes help pay for in your community?
4. What happens if people don't pay their taxes?
5. What is one thing your family uses that taxes help pay for?
6. Why is it important for everyone to help pay taxes?

Section A: Individual Reflection

1. What would happen if no one paid taxes?
2. Why do you think your family might have to help during tax season?

Section B: Vocabulary Building

Matching Puzzle: In the answer column, first write the number and put the correct letters to the side, e.g., 2C.

Definitions	*Words*	*Answers*
A. Money that people and businesses pay to the government to help pay for public services	1) Tax Preparation	
B. Extra money added to the price of things you buy, which goes to the government	2) Tax Season	
C. Extra fees or punishments given when someone breaks a rule or law	3) Filing Taxes	
D. Place or activity where people sell goods or services to make money	4) Taxes	
E. Process of getting your financial information ready to file your taxes	5) Income Tax	
F. The group of people who make and enforce rules for a country or community	6) Sales Tax	
G. Money taken from a person's paid to help pay for government services	7) Property Tax	
H. A group of people living in the same area who share interests and help each other	8) Penalties	
I. The good things or advantages you get from something	9) Deadline	
J. Time of the year when people prepare and file their taxes	10) Benefits	
K. The last date by which something must be done or submitted	11) Business	
L. Money that people pay to the government for owning a home or land	12) Government	
M. Submitting your tax form to the government to report how much money you made and how much tax you owed	13) Community	

Section C: Activities

Word Search Puzzle: Find and circle the financial words hidden in the grid below. Words can go horizontally, vertically, or diagonally.

R	E	M	I	N	D	E	R	A	B	C	D	D			
E	F	G	H	S	T	R	U	C	T	U	R	E		Money	Government
J	C	O	M	M	U	N	I	T	Y	H	I	A		Filing	Taxes
C	O	N	T	R	I	B	U	T	I	O	N	D		Season	Income
H	K	L	M	B	U	S	I	N	E	S	S	L		Sales	Service
A	N	G	O	V	E	R	N	M	E	N	T	I		Contribution	Community
R	O	P	N	I	N	C	O	M	E	Q	A	N		Business	Benefits
G	F	E	E	S	F	I	L	I	N	G	X	E		Require	Reminder
E	R	E	Y	A	S	D	B	A	L	L	E	R		Charges	Deadline
S	S	E	A	S	O	N	E	S	E	Z	S	E		Penalty	Property
P	A	I	D	E	A	R	N	E	R	T	O	P		Structure	Earn
R	L	E	A	R	N	R	E	Q	U	I	R	E		Extra	Fees
E	E	X	A	V	C	V	F	O	X	E	R	N		Prepare	Bills
P	S	T	L	I	P	B	I	L	L	S	A	A		Paid	Earn
A	E	R	A	C	A	E	T	L	A	N	D	L		Owe	Own
R	E	A	W	E	Y	A	S	O	W	N	A	T		Land	Law
E	O	W	E	R	P	R	O	P	E	R	T	Y			

Alternative Activity

- Draw a picture of something that taxes help pay for, like a park or a school.

This case study's conversation helps simply explain taxes, using Jamal and Stacy's family as an example. It also provides questions and activities for students of different ages to learn more about taxes.

Case Study 8: Opening and Running a Small Business

One Saturday, after a long day of running their family-owned grocery store, John and Janet Doe finally sat down for a well-deserved dinner with their three children: Ezekiel, Samira, and Denzel. The aroma of a home-cooked meal filled the air, and the table was set with laughter and love. As they gathered around, the kids were eager to hear about their parents' pay and share their own stories from school. In this cozy moment, the family knew it was the perfect time to connect, share ideas, and discuss the values of hard work and teamwork that made their family business thrive. What engaging conversations would unfold during this special family dinner?

Denzel: "Mom, Dad, I've been thinking a lot lately. I really admire how you've built and run our grocery store. I want to start my own business someday. How did you manage to start and keep the store running, especially with big competitors like Walmart and Giant around?"

John: "That's a great question, Denzel. Starting our grocery store wasn't easy. We knew that competing directly with big retailers would be challenging. So, we focused on offering unique products and personalized customer service that big stores often can't provide.

Janet: "We also made sure to understand what our community needed. By listening to our customers, we could stock items that weren't available elsewhere, giving people a reason to choose our store over the larger ones."

Samira: "But it must have been tough to balance the store and family time, right?"

Janet: "Absolutely. Balancing work and family is always a challenge. We had to set clear boundaries, like dedicating certain hours to the store and others to family time. It required a lot of planning and organization."

Ezekiel: "Did you face any other challenges running the store?"

John: "Yes, many. Managing inventory was one. We had to ensure we stocked the right number of products without buying too much, which could lead to losses. Understanding customer demands was crucial. If we didn't have what customers wanted, they'd go elsewhere."

Janet: "We also had to keep up with various rules called regulations and policies, which sometimes made running the business more complicated than it should be. However, we managed to navigate those challenges by staying informed and adaptable."

Denzel: "It sounds like a lot of work. How did you keep everything running smoothly?"

John: "We couldn't have done it alone. We hired reliable staff and delegated tasks. Trusting our team allowed us to focus on both the business and spending quality time with you all."

Janet: "And we always made time for family. No matter how busy the store got, we ensured we had moments like this dinner to connect and support each other."

Denzel: "I understand now. Running a business takes dedication, understanding your customers, and balancing work with family. Thanks for sharing your experiences."

John: "We're glad you asked, Denzel. Remember, you can achieve your dreams with passion, discipline, focus, and hard work. And we'll always be here to support you."

Learning Objectives

1. Understand what a small business is and how it works. Students will learn that a small business is a store or service run by a person or family to serve their community and earn money.

2. Recognize the importance of customer service and community needs. Students will explore how listening to customers and offering helpful products or services can make a business successful.
3. Learn about the challenges of running a business. Students will be introduced to real-world problems like managing supplies, following rules, and handling competition from bigger stores.
4. Appreciate the need for balance between work and family time. Students will understand that even when people work hard, they must also make time for family and rest.
5. Identify teamwork and planning as key parts of business success. Students will see how working together, sharing tasks, and staying organized helps a business grow and stay strong.

Discussion Questions

1. What are some challenges small businesses face when competing with large retailers?
2. Why is it important for small businesses to understand their community's needs? C) How can setting boundaries help in balancing work and family life?
3. d)Why is delegating tasks important in running a business?
4. What makes small family-owned stores different from big stores like Walmart?
5. Why is spending time with family important, even when running a business?

Section A: Individual Reflection

1. Why do you think John and Janet chose to open their own store instead of working for a big company?
2. How do you feel when your family spends time together after a busy day

Section B: Vocabulary Building

Matching Puzzle: In the answer column, first write the number and put the correct letters to the side, e.g., 2C.

Definitions	*Words*	*Answers*
A. Thinking ahead about what you need to do and how to do it	1) Grocery Store	
B. When people or things are arranged in a neat and orderly way to work well together	2) Community	
C. Rules that people must follow to keep things fair and safe	3) Competition	
D. To give someone a job or pay them to do work for you	4) Planning	
E. A place where people buy food and other things they need for their home	5) Business	
F. Set of rules or guidelines that help people make decisions or do things in a certain way	6) Organization	
G. A list of all the things a store must sell	7) Retail	
H. Being able to change or adjust to new situations or different needs	8) Inventory	
I. Something that is made to be sold, like toys, clothes, or food	9) Challenge	
J. Group of people who live, work, or spend time together and help each other	10) Regulations	
K. Something that is difficult but can be overcome with effort and practice	11) Product	
L. A list of all the things a store must sell	12) Policy	
M. When stores sell things to people for them to use	13) Adaptable	
N. When people make or sell things to earn money	14)Hire	
O. When people or teams try to do better than others to win a game, prize, or goal	15) Staff	

Section C: Activities

Word Search Puzzle: Find and circle the financial words hidden in the grid below. Words can go horizontally, vertically, or diagonally.

U	A	B	O	U	N	D	A	R	I	E	S	E	H
N	C	B	A	L	A	N	C	E	D	E	C	X	A
I	H	S	E	R	V	I	C	E	A	S	F	P	R
Q	I	T	S	T	O	C	K	W	E	R	B	E	D
U	E	O	E	C	A	P	A	B	L	E	U	R	W
E	V	R	R	O	B	A	D	E	C	I	S	I	O
C	E	E	T	U	U	S	A	S	D	E	I	E	R
O	R	G	A	N	I	S	A	T	I	O	N	N	K
M	C	U	D	E	L	I	D	J	U	G	E	C	I
P	H	L	O	N	D	O	A	P	F	E	S	E	N
E	A	A	V	U	E	N	P	R	A	R	S	P	V
T	L	T	E	C	U	S	T	O	M	E	R	R	E
I	L	I	R	P	R	E	A	D	I	O	N	O	N
T	E	O	B	L	E	X	B	U	L	L	O	D	T
I	N	N	U	A	X	E	L	C	Y	E	S	U	O
O	G	E	Y	N	E	R	E	T	A	I	L	C	R
N	E	P	O	L	I	C	Y	R	E	V	E	T	Y
R	E	L	I	A	B	L	E	I	N	F	O	R	M
M	A	N	A	G	E	D	E	C	I	D	E	D	E

Challenge	Customer
Regulation	Product
Policy	Overbuy
Product	Inventory
Passion	Experience
Hard work	Store
Service	Stock
Family	Plan
Boundaries	Reliable
Inform	Manage
Competition	Retail
Organization	Adaptable
Build	Business

Alternative Activity

- Draw a picture of a family working together in their store and spending time together at home.

This case study's conversation and the accompanying questions aim to help students of all ages understand the intricacies of running a family-owned business, the challenges involved, and the importance of balancing work with family commitments.

Case Study 9: Budgeting, Saving, and Emergency Funds

Stella, a devoted mom, was filled with pride as she navigated the joys and challenges of raising her three children: Emmanuela and Noela, twin high school seniors, and her youngest, Josef, who was just in fourth grade. Recently, she received thrilling news—her daughters had earned full academic scholarships to an out-of-state college! While her heart swelled with pride for their achievements, a wave of concern washed over her as she thought about how they would manage their money living on their own. Determined to equip them with the right tools, Stella decided it was time to teach her daughters how to handle their part-time job income wisely. With excitement and intention, she gathered her girls to share valuable lessons about budgeting, saving, and making smart financial choices. What insights would they discover together as they prepared for this new chapter in their lives?

A Family Conversation About Money

STELLA: I'm so proud of you girls for earning scholarships! College will be exciting, but it means making smart financial decisions. Let's talk about budgeting, saving, and creating an emergency fund.

NOELA: What's budgeting?

STELLA: A budget is a plan for managing your money. It shows how much you earn, spend, and save. For example, if you earn $200 a week, you might spend $50 on groceries, save $100 for goals, and keep $50 for fun. A budget helps you avoid running out of money.

JOSEF: Do I need a budget too?

STELLA: Yes! Even with your $10 allowance, you can plan to save $5 for a toy and spend $5 on snacks. It's about deciding how to use your money wisely.

EMMANUELA: What if I want something that's not in my budget?

STELLA: That's where saving comes in. Sometimes, you must make sacrifices to reach bigger goals. Instead of spending all your money on small things like coffee, save for something bigger, like a laptop or a trip. Prioritize needs over wants.

NOELA: How do I know what I need and what's a want?

STELLA: Needs are essentials like food, housing, or school supplies. Wants are things you'd like but can live without, like a fancy dress or a new phone. Always handle needs first.

JOSEF: What about saving for emergencies?

STELLA: An emergency fund is money set aside for unexpected events, like car repairs or medical bills. It's a safety net. But remember, not everything is an emergency. Buying a video game isn't!

EMMANUELA: How much should we save for emergencies?

STELLA: Experts recommend saving three to six months of living expenses, but starting small helps. Even $500 can make a difference.

NOELA: What if we can't save after paying for everything else?

STELLA: That's why budgeting is key. Track your spending and cut back where you can, like cooking at home instead of eating out. Small changes add up over time.

JOSEF: This sounds like a lot to remember.

STELLA: It might feel that way, but here's a simple summary:

- Create a budget to plan your spending and saving.
- Save regularly for goals and emergencies.
- Always prioritize needs before wants.

EMMANUELA: Thanks, Mom. I'm ready to start budgeting and saving.

NOELA: Me too. I want to manage my money well in college.

STELLA: I'm proud of you both. Remember, I'm here to help if you have questions.

Learning Objectives

1. Understand what a budget is and why it is important. Students will learn that a budget is a simple plan to help manage money—how much is earned, spent, and saved.
2. Learn to separate needs from wants. Students will practice identifying the difference between things they must have (like food and school supplies) and things they would like to have (like games or treats).
3. Recognize the value of saving for future goals. Students will understand that saving money helps them buy bigger or more important things later by making small sacrifices today.
4. Discover the purpose of an emergency fund. Students will learn that setting money aside for unexpected problems—like a broken bike or doctor visit—is a smart and helpful habit.
5. Identify small daily habits that support good money choices. Students will explore simple ways to save, like skipping small purchases or tracking how they spend their money.

Discussion Questions

1. What is a budget, and why is it important?
2. Why is it important to save money?
3. c)What is an emergency fund, and how can it help you?
4. d)How can you tell the difference between a need and a want?
5. What's one way you can create a budget with your allowance?
6. Why is it important to save for emergencies?
7. Can you think of something that's a need and something that's a want?

Section A: Individual Reflection

1. What would you do if you saved $20 but saw a toy you wanted that cost $15?
2. Would you buy the toy or save your money? Why?
3. How could you help your family save money at home?

Section B: Vocabulary Building

Matching Puzzle: In the answer column, first write the number and put the correct letters to the side, e.g., 2C.

Definitions	*Words*	*Answers*
A. Money Saved for unexpected expenses like fixing a car or a doctor's visit	1) Scholarship	
B. Money set aside for later instead of spending it now	2) Achievement	
C. A person who knows a lot about a particular subject or skill	3) Money Management	
D. Something that is most important and needs to be done first	4) College	
E. Money for school that helps students pay for their education	5) Emergency Fund	
F. How you plan and use your money wisely	6) Savings	
G. Use your money to buy something	7) Financial Decision	
H. Get money by working or doing something	8) Budgeting	
I. Giving up something you want now for something more important later	9) Earn	
J. Things that are essential for living, like food, water, and shelter	10) Spend	
K. Things you would like to have but can live without them. e.g., toys and candy	11) Track	
L. Thing you want to achieve or reach in the future.	12) Decision Making	
M. The process of choosing what to do from different options	13) Sacrifices	
N. To keep a record of something, like how much money you have or buy	14) Goals	
O. Something you succeed at after working hard	15)Priority	
P. A choice you make about how to spend or save your money	16)Needs	
Q. Planning how to spend and save your money wisely	17) Wants	
R. A school where you go after high school to learn more and prepare for a job	18)Expert	

Section C: Activities

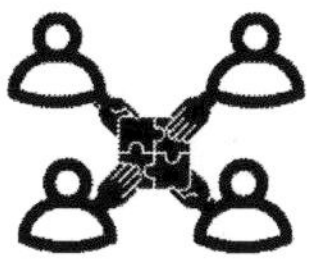

Word Search Puzzle: Find and circle the financial words hidden in the grid below. Words can go horizontally, vertically, or diagonally.

R	F	I	N	A	N	C	E	S	P	I	C	A	S	I	R	P
E	E	S	S	E	N	T	I	A	L	X	E	E	A	M	O	R
C	E	R	T	I	S	U	M	M	A	R	Y	E	V	P	M	I
O	S	E	R	T	E	X	P	E	N	S	E	S	I	O	P	O
M	D	S	A	C	R	I	F	I	C	E	S	O	N	R	O	R
M	A	C	H	I	E	V	E	M	E	N	T	N	G	T	T	I
E	N	H	S	M	A	R	T	A	T	T	E	E	S	T	E	T
N	G	O	A	L	S	B	O	N	C	O	L	L	E	G	E	Y
D	O	L	U	V	O	U	R	A	L	L	O	W	A	N	C	E
S	D	A	F	U	N	D	E	G	R	O	C	E	R	I	E	S
E	A	R	N	I	N	G	N	E	E	D	S	V	O	B	U	T
X	E	S	D	E	G	E	N	M	O	N	E	Y	O	K	K	C
P	U	H	S	D	G	T	W	E	E	K	D	F	H	I	O	R
E	Q	I	F	U	N	D	I	N	C	O	M	E	G	G	H	E
R	S	P	E	N	D		X	T	R	A	C	K	D	S	O	A
T	W	A	N	T	S	P	R	I	O	R	I	T	I	Z	E	T
S	D	E	C	I	S	I	O	N	E	X	P	E	R	T	V	E

Scholarship	Achievement
Management	Income
Sacrifice	Needs
Spend	Wants
Week	Goals
Earning	Prioritize
Budget	Smart
Groceries	Experts
Decision	Essential
Plan	Summary
Expenses	Recommend
Money	Track
Savings	College
Fund	Priority
Expert	Finance
Import	Create

Alternative Activities

1. Draw a picture of three things you want to save money for. Label them as "need" or "want."
2. Write down how you would divide $10 if you wanted to spend some and save the rest.

This case study shows how Stella prepares Emmanuela, Noela, and Josef to make smart financial decisions. By learning how to budget, save, and create emergency funds, they'll be better prepared to handle their money wisely in the future.

YOUNANCE FINANCIAL LITERACY

Case Study 10: Investing and Growing Wealth

Stam, a knowledgeable financial advisor, dedicated his career to helping people grow their money through smart investing. One bright Saturday morning, his curious kids—Ivo (16), Mark (12), and Esther (nine)— approached him with eager eyes, asking if he could explain the basics of investing to them. Seeing their enthusiasm, Stam felt a spark of excitement himself. It was the perfect opportunity to share what he loved most. Gathering around the kitchen table, he prepared to break down complex concepts into simple, relatable ideas. He aimed to inspire their understanding of how money could work for them with a mix of fun examples and engaging stories. What valuable lessons would his children learn about investing that could set them on a path to financial empowerment?

A Family Conversation About Investments and Financial Growth

IVO: "Dad, I recently watched this gentleman on YouTube talk about Investing. What is investing?"

STAM: "Investing helps your money grow over time. Instead of keeping money in a piggy bank or savings account, you can put it into things like the stock market, bonds, or Cryptocurrency to earn more. That's how people build wealth."

MARK: "What's the stock market?"

STAM: "It's like a big store where you can buy pieces of companies called stocks. If the company does well, the stock's value increases, and your money grows."

ESTHER: "What about cryptocurrency?"

STAM: "Cryptocurrency is digital money, like Bitcoin. It's secure because of blockchain technology, but it's risky since its value changes a lot quickly.

IVO: "Is investing only for adults?"

STAM: "No! The earlier you start, the better. With compounding interest, your money grows faster over time. For example, if you invest $100 monthly at age 18, you could have over $20,000 by age 30. Waiting until 30 means less growth, even with the same amount of time."

MARK: "What should I invest in?"

STAM: "Stocks are one option. Bonds are safer but grow more slowly. Mutual or index funds are great because they spread your money across many investments, reducing risk."

ESTHER: "Is saving in a bank better?"

STAM: "Saving in a bank is a good start, but banks offer low interest, so your money grows slowly. Investing increases your money faster, but it comes with risks. The key is balancing safer options, like bonds, with riskier ones, like stocks.

IVO: "What's a 401(k)?"

STAM: "A 401(k) is a retirement plan where you save part of your paycheck, and it grows over time. Some companies even match your savings like free money! There's also the 529 Plan for college savings." Mark: "This sounds complicated."

STAM: "It might at first, but start small. Save a little each week and watch it grow. When you're older, invest part of your income. The earlier you start, the more your money will grow."

ESTHER: "Can you help us when we're ready?"

STAM: "Of course! Investing is like planting a tree—it takes time, but if you care about it, it will grow big and strong.

Learning Objectives

1. Understand what investing means and why people do it. Students will learn that investing is a way to grow their money over time by putting it into things like stocks, bonds, or funds.

2. Identify basic types of investments. Students will be introduced to simple investment options such as stocks, bonds, mutual funds, and cryptocurrencies in easy-to-understand terms.
3. Explore the concept of risk and reward in investing. Students will learn that some investments are riskier but may grow faster, while others are safer but grow more slowly.
4. Recognize the importance of starting early and letting money grow over time. Students will understand that the earlier they begin saving and investing, the more their money can grow through compounding interest.
5. Learn how to balance saving and investing. Students will discover that both saving (for safety) and investing (for growth) are important for building wealth and reaching future goals.

Discussion Questions

1. What is investing, and why is it important?
2. What's the difference between saving and investing?
3. Why is it important to start investing early?
4. d)What does it mean to "buy a stock"?
5. Why is it better to save money instead of spending it all at once?
6. What would you save for if you started investing today?

Section A: Individual Reflection

1. Imagine you had $10 to save or invest. Would you put it in a piggy bank or a savings account, or invest it in something like stocks? Why?
2. Why do you think it's important to save money for the future?

Section B: Vocabulary Building

Matching Puzzle: In the answer column, first write the number and put the correct letters to the side, e.g., 2C.

Definitions	*Words*	*Answers*
A. A container used to save coins and money in it	1) 529 Plan	
B. A place where shares of companies are bought and sold	2) Paycheck	
C. Money paid to an employee for their work	3) Financial Advisor	
D. Digital money that uses encryption for security	4) Investing	
E. An organization that sells goods or services	5) Piggybank	
F. A savings account for education expenses	6) Stock Market	
G. Money that exists only in electronic form	7) Bonds	
H. Tools and machines that help solve problems	8) Cryptocurrency	
I. Interest that is calculated on the initial principal and on the accumulated interest	9) Wealth	
J. A type of mutual fund that tracks a specific market index	10) Stocks	
K. A contract giving the right to buy or sell an asset at a set price	11) Company	
L. A retirement savings plan sponsored by an employer	12) Digital Money	
M. Putting money into something to earn more money	13) Blockchain	
N. The abundance of valuable resources or money	14) Technology	
O. A person who puts money into something to make more money from it	15) Risky	
P. Involving the chance of loss or danger	16) Compound Interest	
Q) Loans made to companies or governments that pay interest	17) Mutual Fund	
R) A secure digital ledger of transactions	18) Index Fund	
S) Shares that represent ownership in a company	19) Option	
T) A professional who gives money advice to clients	20) 401(k)	
U) A pool of money from many investors to buy stocks and bonds	21) Investors	

Section C: Activities

Word Search Puzzle: Find and circle the financial words hidden in the grid below. Words can go horizontally, vertically, or diagonally.

5	2	9	P	L	A	N	E	S	T	4	0	1	K	O	T
E	R	P	I	G	G	Y	B	A	N	K	O	T	E	A	R
B	I	N	T	E	R	E	S	T	B	A	L	A	N	C	E
I	I	W	E	A	L	T	H	A	O	W	G	O	K	C	A
T	N	I	N	S	P	I	R	E	N	E	R	N	P	O	S
C	V	C	O	M	P	O	U	N	D	R	O	E	I	U	U
O	E	R	D	I	G	I	T	A	L	I	W	S	G	N	R
I	S	Y	A	U	D	I	T	S	T	O	R	E	G	T	Y
N	T	P	A	Y	C	H	E	C	K	T	A	S	Y	R	O
O	S	T	O	C	K	M	A	R	K	E	T	T	B	E	T
B	L	O	C	K	C	H	A	I	N	V	T	O	A	A	E
T	E	C	H	N	O	L	O	G	Y	A	E	C	N	R	C
O	E	U	R	E	V	A	L	U	E	L	N	K	K	I	H
P	L	R	E	I	N	D	E	X	F	U	N	D	E	S	N
T	O	R	V	I	N	C	O	M	E	E	T	I	T	K	O
I	S	E	A	S	O	N	A	D	V	I	S	O	R	Y	L
O	E	N	M	U	T	U	A	L	F	U	N	D	I	N	O
N	R	C	O	M	P	A	N	I	E	S	B	O	X	G	G
A	Y	Y	B	A	L	A	N	C	E	P	H	O	N	E	Y

Technology	Stock market
Blockchain	Companies
Season	Paycheck
Option	Piggybank
Balance	Bond
Store	Index Fund
Mutual Fund	Value
Digital	Bitcoin
Grow	Wealth
Risky	Value
Advisor	Invest
Account	Interest
Technology	Stock
529 Plan	401k
Phone	Treasury
Compound	Cryptocurrency
Inspire	Audit

Alternative Activity

- Draw a picture of a tree and label it "My Money Tree." Write down three things you would save for or invest your money in as the tree grows.

This case study introduces Ivo, Mark, and Esther to the basics of investing while showing how starting early and understanding risk versus reward can set them up for a strong financial future.

About the Author

Born in Bamenda, Cameroon, and raised in Yaoundé, Pearl was privileged to be given the opportunity by his siblings to pursue his dreams in the United States. With a Graduate Diploma in Financial Planning and a passionate career in the financial industry, he realized his true calling: empowering the next generation.

When Pearl isn't coaching on the soccer field, he's dedicating himself to educating and training young minds in financial literacy—arming them with the knowledge and skills to succeed. His journey is a testament to resilience, purpose, and a commitment to transforming lives through education.

Why I Created YOUNANCE: Empowering Teens with Financial Literacy

When I moved to this country, I thought landing a job would automatically solve my money problems. Even with a background in finance, I quickly learned that knowing about money isn't just a math thing; it's about habits, choices, and mindset.

While working in the finance industry, I saw a clear divide: some families teach their children about money from a young age—opening savings accounts, explaining credit, practicing patience, and setting them up for success. Others, especially in communities of color, lacked that early guidance, often seeking credit without understanding how it works or how to manage it responsibly. That is usually because they have no time to spend with their kids, as they often work two or three jobs to make ends meet.

All of us have made mistakes with money. What matters is the willingness to learn and grow from those mistakes. That's why I created YOUNANCE (an abbreviated form of "Your Finance"), a resource to make financial literacy accessible, relatable, and empowering to young people.

My mission is to inspire teens to start healthy money habits now—talking openly about finances, understanding how money works, and preparing for a future where they control their financial destiny. When young people learn these lessons early, they can break cycles, build confidence, and create a legacy of financial wellness.

What qualifies me to teach financial literacy?

I've made big mistakes with money. Instead of making excuses, I owned it, then committed to learning. Today, I'm applying those lessons and seeing the power of financial knowledge firsthand.

Imagine the impact if our next generation learns from our mistakes and is equipped to make smarter choices. YOUNANCE is about giving our children the tools to break cycles, seize opportunities, and build a stronger future. Together, we can create a legacy of financial empowerment—starting today. Let's make that change happen.

Made in the USA
Monee, IL
05 November 2026

67811033R10042